THIS BOOK BELONGS TO

Ms. Messing

name

EXTINCT FOR 65 MILLION YEARS, THEY'RE BACK!

Jurassic Park is a totally unique "zoo" located on Nublar Island, about 125 miles (200 km) off the coast of Costa Rica, in Central America. The fulfillment of five years work, is a dream come true for John Hammond, a businessman who made his fortune creating theme parks and zoos around the world.

Imagine an island covered with lush vegetation and inhabited by . . .
LIVE DINOSAURS!

HOW JURASSIC PARK BEGAN

First, paleontologists discovered dinosaur-age fossil mosquitoes (blood-sucking insects) preserved in chunks of amber. The insects' stomachs still contained the preserved blood of dinosaurs they bit more than 65 million years ago. Genetic scientists were then able to remove the ancient dinosaur DNA (the genetic code that acts as a blueprint for creating life) and, with the help of powerful computers, they created living dinosaur embryos.

Dinosaurs are a group of ancient reptiles that lived on the Earth long before human beings appeared. No one had ever seen a living dinosaur before . . . until now!

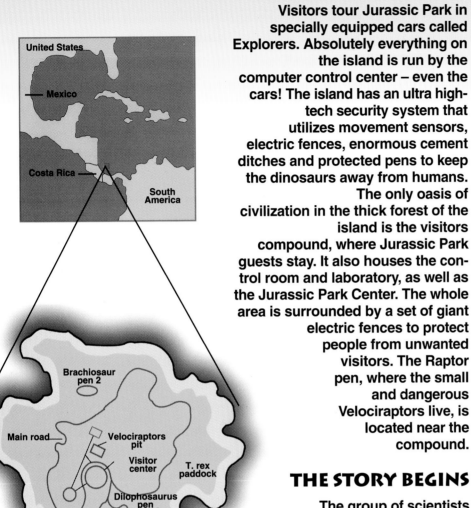

United States

Mexico

Costa Rica

South America

Brachiosaur pen 2

Main road

Velociraptors pit

Visitor center

T. rex paddock

Dilophosaurus pen

Dock

Vista view

Access road

Helipad

Brachiosaur pen 1

Visitors tour Jurassic Park in specially equipped cars called Explorers. Absolutely everything on the island is run by the computer control center – even the cars! The island has an ultra high-tech security system that utilizes movement sensors, electric fences, enormous cement ditches and protected pens to keep the dinosaurs away from humans.

The only oasis of civilization in the thick forest of the island is the visitors compound, where Jurassic Park guests stay. It also houses the control room and laboratory, as well as the Jurassic Park Center. The whole area is surrounded by a set of giant electric fences to protect people from unwanted visitors. The Raptor pen, where the small and dangerous Velociraptors live, is located near the compound.

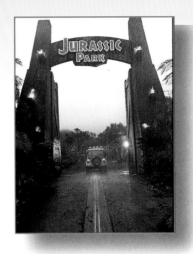

THE STORY BEGINS

The group of scientists and visitors arriving at Jurassic Park are about to be the first to tour the park and see living dinosaurs, before the official opening.

The weather is beautiful now, but a tropical storm is heading for the island at lightning speed.

Everything seems fine, but things are about to go very wrong . . .

HERE ARE THE EIGHT CHARACTERS WHO WILL EXPLORE JURASSIC PARK WITH YOU

DR. ELLIE SATTLER

Dr. Ellie Sattler is a paleobotanist, a scientist who studies fossil plants. She's come to Jurassic Park to assist Dr. Grant with the inspection.

TIM

Tim is the nine-year-old grandson of John Hammond. A big dinosaur buff, he's on the island to visit his grandpa — and Dr. Grant, his hero.

DR. ALAN GRANT

Dr. Alan Grant, a paleontologist who studies the skeletons and behavior of carnivorous dinosaurs, has been invited to Jurassic Park to inspect the facilities before the official park opening.

JOHN HAMMOND

John Hammond is a billionaire business-man who accom-plished his dream to build Jurassic Park. Totally obsessed by dinosaurs, he has invented a new kind of theme park. His company, InGen Corporation, created Jurassic Park and all its dinosaurs.

ALEXIS (LEX)

Lex is Tim's 12-year-old sister. She's as crazy about computers as Tim is about dinosaurs, and she has a crush on Dr. Grant.

DR. IAN MALCOLM

Dr. Ian Malcolm is a mathematical genius here to inspect the operations. However, he doesn't believe that science can always control complex natural systems. He's certain that something will eventually go wrong with the park.

ROBERT MULDOON

Robert Muldoon is the island game warden. Although he's worked with dangerous wild animals for years, he doesn't trust the dinosaurs — especially the Velociraptors.

DENNIS NEDRY

Dennis Nedry programmed all the computer systems in Jurassic Park. He secretly decided to sell frozen dinosaur embryos to a rival company for a lot of money. To sneak the embryos off the island, he uses the computer to turn off the Jurassic Park security system. Unfortunately, his program eventually shuts down all island control systems. Now none of the electric fences are operational and the dinosaurs will soon discover that they can escape!

NOW, IT'S TIME TO MEET ONE OF THE INHABITANTS OF JURASSIC PARK . . .

Lex, Tim, Dr. Grant, Dr. Sattler and Dr. Malcolm have started their tour of Jurassic Park in two remote-controlled Explorers, with Lex and Tim in the front vehicle. They are thrilled to see living dinosaurs in a natural environment. The excitement builds as they approach the Tyrannosaurus pen. The vehicles stop and wait, but no Tyrannosaurus appears. Becoming impatient, Dr. Grant, who studied the fossilized bones of Tyrannosaurus rex, gets out of the Explorer to have a closer look through the fence. Everyone else decides to follow. Tyrannosaurus is nowhere to be seen, but what's that over there? Suddenly, they see the form of an animal lying down, outside the Tyrannosaurus pen. What could this strange animal be?

TRICERATOPS

Meaning of name:
Three-horned face

Lived: 67 to 65 million years ago

Herbivorous, Ornithischian Dinosaur

Family Ceratopsidae

Found in North America

First discovered in 1888,
Converse County, Wyoming, USA

Scientifically described by Dr. O.C. Marsh in 1889

Maximum known body size:
30 feet / 9 meters long, 10 feet / 3 meters tall

Skull length:
6 feet / 1.8 meters

Weight:
5,000 pounds / 2.5 metric tonnes

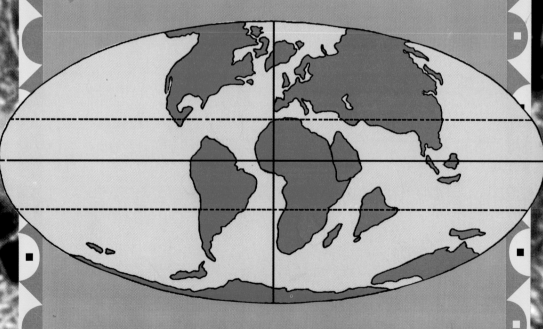

This map shows the arrangement of the continents during the time of Triceratops.

Over the past hundred years, scientists have described more than 16 species of Triceratops, most from the small area of Montana, Wyoming and South Dakota. Recently, two scientists re-examined all the Triceratops fossils in museums around the world. They decided there was only one species of Triceratops (horridus) and that all the other species belonged to it. They suggested that all the other species were created because of minor differences in the skull shapes due to variations in the ways each animal grew during its life. Humans show similar growth differences.

The size of a full-sized adult Triceratops compared to a six-foot (1.85 m) human.

It's a Triceratops, a plant-eating dinosaur that will not hurt them. Triceratops looks almost asleep. The children run towards it, excited to get close to a real prehistoric animal.

Horned dinosaurs, or ceratopsians as scientists know them, were a group of dinosaurs identified by a frill of bone around the back of their skulls and by the horns that most had on their faces. Ancestors of the ceratopsians migrated from Asia into North America through Alaska and northern Canada. Ceratopsians, at present, seem to be found only in North America. Horned dinosaurs likely migrated back to Asia, but scientists have not yet found their fossils there.

Triceratops has been found in the United States, Canada, and Mexico. Interestingly, it is very unusual to find a Triceratops skeleton, but skulls are found fairly often. There are perhaps two reasons for this: the environment where the Triceratops lived, and the weight of its colossal head. When a Triceratops died, its body would be carried away by one of the numerous rivers. The heavy head would eventually separate and sink to the bottom of the river, while the lighter body would float away — leaving the skull to be buried in river sand.

Near the Triceratops stands Dr. Harding, the park veterinarian. As everyone moves in closer, Dr. Sattler notices the animal's pupils appear dilated. The Triceratops is sick and the veterinarian has administered a tranquilizer so he can examine it safely.

This map shows where the bones of Triceratops have been found.

Dr. Grant is overwhelmed! All he has ever seen of dinosaurs were the dry fossil bones — and now he is the first paleontologist to see and touch a living, breathing dinosaur! What's more, it's a Triceratops, his favorite dinosaur since he was a little boy!

It is believed that all dinosaurs, like birds and most reptiles, laid eggs to reproduce. Because fossil baby bones are rarely found inside, few of the many existing types of dinosaur eggs can actually be matched to known dinosaurs.

At present, there are no known Triceratops eggs, however eggs from an Asian cousin Protoceratops are well known. The eggs were laid in a spiral pattern and then covered with sand to incubate.

This illustration is of a Protoceratops nest.

It is believed that dinosaurs took care of their young, so one can imagine a mother Triceratops standing guard over its nest — protecting the eggs from the many small meat-eating dinosaurs.

Dinosaur eggs don't look like the giant ones we see in cartoons. The mother dinosaur would have trouble laying them if they were very large. Also, large eggs must have thick shells to support their weight. The thicker the shell, the harder it is for babies to push their way out. You could have a giant egg, but it wouldn't be much good if the baby needed a hammer to get out. Eggs, whether dinosaur or bird, never get much bigger than a football.

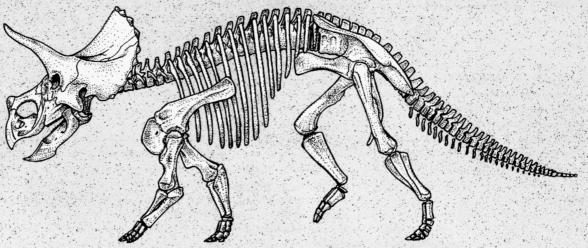

The skeleton is shown from the side and above so you can get a good understanding of the animal's shape.

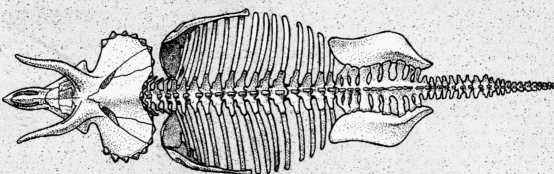

Notice how large the skull is in comparison to the body.

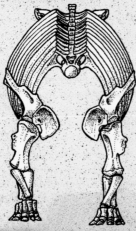

Front

These two illustrations show the skeleton from the front and back. We have removed parts of the body so we can see the animal's true shape.

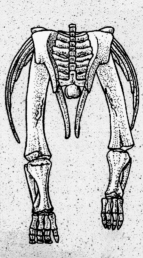

Back

and the muscles that cover its bones.

The powerful muscles of Triceratops allowed it to both hold up its
weight and be agile when protecting itself from predators. Every
animal with a backbone uses its hard skeleton to anchor its muscles.
Scientists can reconstruct how dinosaurs looked by examining fossil
bones for the marks left by the muscle attachments, and by
comparing them to the modern cousins of the
dinosaur — crocodiles and birds.

The heavy head of Triceratops was attached to its body by strong neck muscles and an amazing ball-and-socket joint at the back of the skull. This joint looks a lot like the trailer hitch system we use today to attach cars to trailers. At the back of the skull is a large round bone that fits into a cup-like socket at the top of the neck. Like a trailer hitch, this joint allowed the Triceratops skull to be flexible while firmly supporting its weight.

Strong muscles let Triceratops pull its head up and down at great speed.

Scientists are sure Triceratops used its head and horns to protect it from predators like Tyrannosaurus. The horns and sharp beak were probably sufficient to drive off most attacks, but fossil Triceratops bones have been found carrying the marks of Tyrannosaurus teeth.

Looking in the mouth of the Triceratops, Dr. Sattler notices unusual sores on its tongue. She calls over Dr. Grant, who kneels to examine the animal. What could have caused these symptoms?

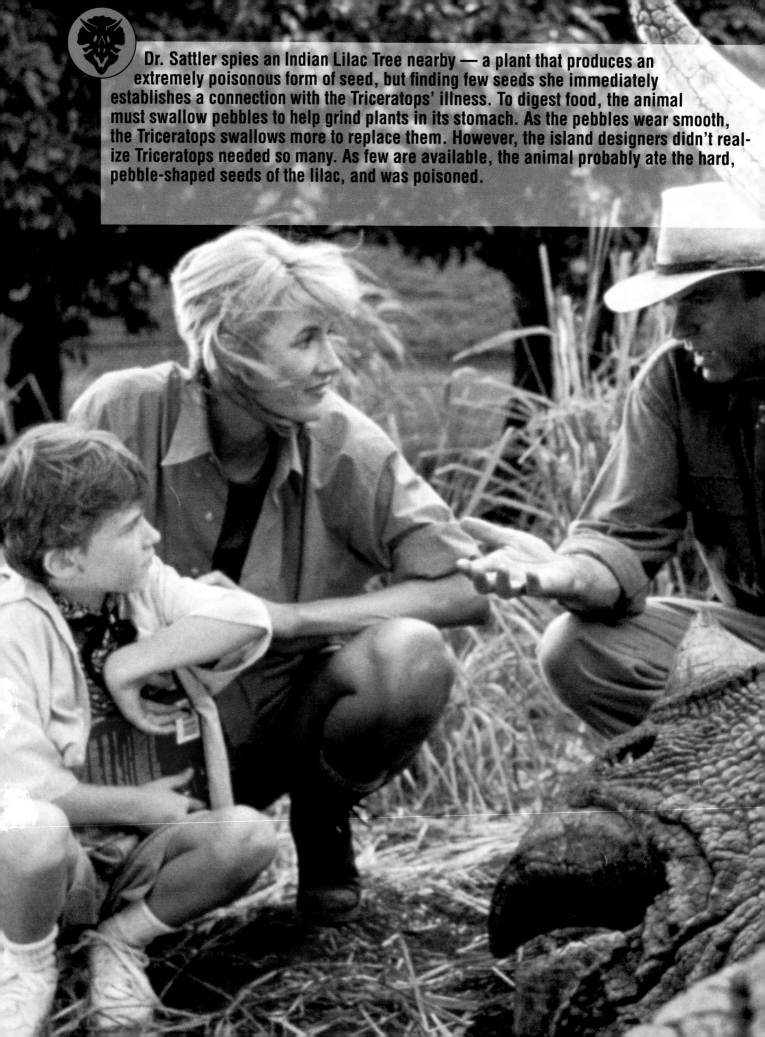

Dr. Sattler spies an Indian Lilac Tree nearby — a plant that produces an extremely poisonous form of seed, but finding few seeds she immediately establishes a connection with the Triceratops' illness. To digest food, the animal must swallow pebbles to help grind plants in its stomach. As the pebbles wear smooth, the Triceratops swallows more to replace them. However, the island designers didn't realize Triceratops needed so many. As few are available, the animal probably ate the hard, pebble-shaped seeds of the lilac, and was poisoned.

The most obvious feature of the Triceratops is the three big horns on its face. The two largest are above each eye, and there is a smaller horn on the tip of the nose. As large as each of these bone horns are, an even larger non-bone horn was on top of them when the animals were alive. Like almost all the other soft parts on a dinosaur's body, they were not preserved when the animal died.

The brain of Triceratops was not large, but was capable of controlling the complex behavior scientists believe it had. Dinosaurs have long been labeled stupid, because of the relatively small size of their brains in comparison to their bodies. It is now believed that, though dinosaurs were no philosophers, they were at least as smart as birds are today. No group of animals could rule the earth for 150 million years and be that stupid.

Like most plant-eating dinosaurs, Triceratops had rows of powerful cutting and grinding teeth along its jaws. The sharp beak at the front was used for peeling bark and cutting branches. The plants were then passed back to the teeth by a long flexible tongue.

Conifers

Most people are surprised to learn that dinosaurs ate rough plants like evergreens and that these pine trees evolved in tropical regions over 200 million years ago.

Cycads

Cycads are an ancient group of fern-like plants that survive in tropical areas even today. They have large round fibrous stumps with bunches of green branches growing out of the top.

Flowering Plants

During the late part of the dinosaur age, the Cretaceous period, flowering plants came into existence. As the term "flowering plants" refers to all plants that use flowers to reproduce, this includes not only plants like daisies and roses, but also most of the trees we know today.

Deciding it's time to leave, Dr. Grant and Dr. Malcolm walk back and get into their Explorer, and Lex and Tim climb into theirs. They still want to see the Tyrannosaurus. Dr. Sattler decides to stay behind with the veterinarian to examine the Triceratops more thoroughly. She will return to the Park Center later with the park warden who should join them soon. She has no idea yet how important it was to stay behind . . .

DINOSAUR EGGS

To reproduce, dinosaurs laid eggs from which baby dinosaurs
hatched. You can make your own dinosaur nest!

You need :
Eggshells
Paint
Modeling clay
Coarse salt
A bowl

Use half eggshells (don't waste the eggs) and wash them carefully

Paint the eggshells (handle very carefully, they're fragile!), and let them dry.

Make baby dinosaurs out of modeling clay and place them in the half shells.

Pour about an inch (2 cm) of coarse salt in a deep plate or shallow bowl and arrange the baby
dinosaurs. Now you have a dinosaur nest!

Bipedal	An animal that walks on its two back legs.
Ceratopsian	A family of dinosaurs that had horns and a bony frill on its head.
Dinosaur	An extinct group of land-dwelling animals closely related to birds and reptiles.
DNA	The short name for the genetic blueprints that determine the structure of a living organism.
Embryo	A fertilized animal egg.
Fossil	Any preserved evidence of ancient life.
Herbivore	Any animal which gets its food energy from eating plants.
Ornithischian	One of the two main groups of dinosaurs; defined by the position of the bones in their hips. The bone positions resemble those of modern birds, therefore they are called "bird-hipped" or ornithischian.
Paleobotanist	A scientist who specifically studies fossil plants.
Paleontologist	A scientist who studies the evidence of ancient life.
Predator	Any organism that pursues or hunts animals for food.
Protoceratopsian	A family of small dinosaurs that gave rise to the Ceratopsians.
Quadrupedal	An animal that walks on all four legs.
Tranquilizer	A form of drug used to knock out or calm down an animal .
Veterinarian	A doctor who takes care of the health of animals.

Text
Lucie Duchesne and Andrew Leitch

Research
Andrew Leitch

Cover Illustration
Michel-Thomas Poulin

Illustrations
PaleoImage Ltd.

Art Direction
Studio de la Montagne
Louis C. Hébert

Desktop Publishing
Benoît Lafond and Line Godbout

Produced by
Group Potential Inc.

With photos from the movie
Jurassic Park

From a screenplay by
Michael Crichton et David Koepp

Based on a novel by
Michael Crichton